PATIENCE

by Beverly Fiday
illustrated by Christina Rigo

THE CHILD'S WORLD

ELGIN, ILLINOIS 60120

Distributed by Childrens Press, 1224 West Van Buren Street, Chicago, Illinois 60607.

Library of Congress Cataloging in Publication Data

Fiday, Beverly, 1951-
    Patience.

    (What is it?)
    Summary: Depicts times when we must exercise patience: finishing a jigsaw puzzle, waiting for our birthdays, and learning how to tie shoes.
    1. Patience—Juvenile literature.   [1. Patience.
2. Conduct of life]   I. Wiles, Carol, 1953-
II. Rigo, Christina Ljungren, ill.   III. Title.
IV. Series.
BJ1533.P3F53   1986   179'.9   86-12984
ISBN 0-89565-358-3

2 3 4 5 6 7 8 9 10 11 12 R 93 92 91 90 89 88 87

PATIENCE

It's raining,
  It's raining,
    It's raining again.

Won't it ever stop?
Katy wants to go with me
To play on the swings
In the park.
But. . .

It's raining,
  It's raining,
    It's raining again.

It's raining everywhere,
So Katy can't come play with me.
And I can't play
With her.

Mom says, "Have patience. The rain
will stop."

—Penny Anderson
from *Feeling Frustrated*

What is patience?

Patience is waiting for your turn to
jump rope.

Patience is waiting for the seed
you planted to grow into a flower.

When, with Mom, you have to wait
in line at the grocery check-out,
patience is trying not to complain.

AISLE 3

9

When you are all finished buttoning your
sweater. . .and then find that you've
put a button in the wrong hole. . .it takes
patience to try again.

And working until you finish a jigsaw
puzzle can take a lot of patience.

Patience is not complaining when you
go for a walk with your little brother —
and have to take small steps.

Also, it's reading his favorite story
over and over and over again.

Wrapping a birthday present for Dad
takes patience.

And waiting until it's YOUR birthday
takes even more!

Learning how to tie your shoes takes
patience.

So does teaching Buster to sit.

"A little patience" is what Mom asks you to have, when you're ready to go to the swimming pool — and she's still dressing your little brother.

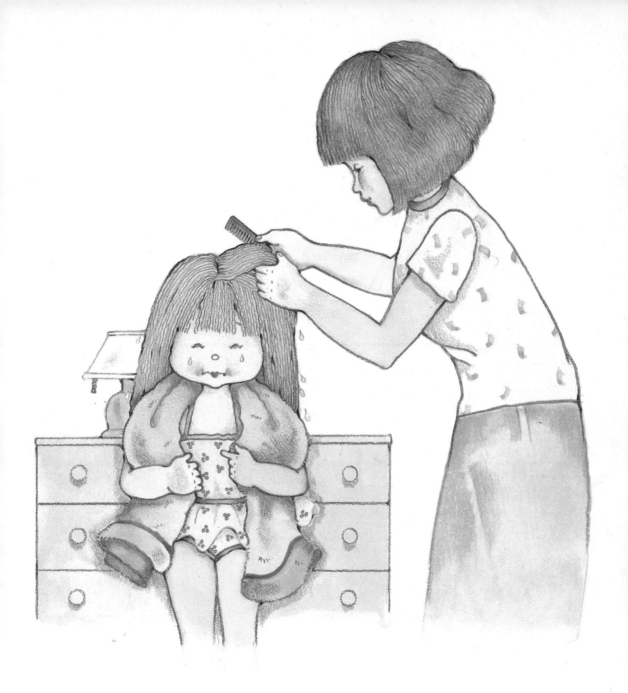

And when you're through swimming, it
takes patience to stand still while Mom
combs the tangles out of your hair.

When the car is packed and everyone is ready to leave for a picnic, patience is waiting for Mom while she goes back inside to get a blanket.

And when you get to the picnic grounds,
patience is waiting until the fire is hot
enough to roast the wieners.

When you're going on a long trip,
patience is waiting for the drive
to end.

When you've moved to a new house,
waiting to make friends with the
children next door takes patience.

Patience is waiting to open your
presents on Christmas morning.

Most of all, patience is waiting to be "big enough."

In what other ways can you show
patience?

About the Author:

Beverly Fiday has had many years of experience working with children. A graduate of Northern Illinois University, Mrs. Fiday is a remedial reading teacher. She has taught reading to children in grades one through eight. In addition, over the last four years, Mrs. Fiday has done free-lance writing. Mrs. Fiday and her husband live in Joliet, Illinois. They have two daughters.

About the Artist:

Christina Ljungren Rigo graduated from Wittenberg University in Springfield, Ohio, with a B.S.A., and first worked as an account executive for an art studio. Subsequently, she was employed as a children's illustrator for a greeting card company. For the last three years, Mrs. Rigo has been a free-lance illustrator. She is married to an illustrator and presently resides in Evanston, Illinois.